BOOKS BY

Mark Strand

DARKER   1970

REASONS FOR MOVING   1968

SLEEPING WITH ONE EYE OPEN   1964

DARKER

DARKER

Poems by

MARK STRAND

*I have a key
so I open the door and walk in.
It is dark and I walk in.
It is darker and I walk in.*

ATHENEUM

New York

1970

The poems in this book have appeared in the following magazines: CON-CERNING POETRY, FIELD, HARPER'S, KAYAK, THE NEW YORKER, THE NEW YORK REVIEW OF BOOKS, THE NEW REPUBLIC, POETRY, POETRY NORTHWEST, STAND, TRANSITION, TRI-QUARTERLY.

The following poems appeared originally in THE NEW YORKER: *Breath, Letter, Tomorrow, The Remains, The Hill, The Sleep, The Recovery, The Dance, The Good Life, The Dress, My Life, The Guardian, Not Dying.*

The following poems appeared originally in POETRY: *Black Maps, Seven Poems.*

The first two stanzas of *The One Song* are taken from a ninth-century Chinese poem called *Resignation,* as it appears in Arthur Waley's CHINESE POETRY.

The author wishes to thank The National Endowment for The Arts and The Rockefeller Foundation for grants which helped him to complete this book.

Library of Congress catalog card number 70–124966
Published simultaneously in Canada by McClelland and Stewart Ltd.
Manufactured in the United States of America by
Kingsport Press, Inc., Kingsport, Tennessee
Designed by Kathleen Carey
First Edition

For

ANTONIA

and for

RICHARD

Contents

I   *Giving Myself Up*

THE NEW POETRY HANDBOOK   3
BREATH   5
LETTER   6
GIVING MYSELF UP   7
TOMORROW   8
THE ROOM   9
NOSTALGIA   10
THE REMAINS   11
THE DANCE   12
THE GOOD LIFE   13
THE DRESS   14
THE GUARDIAN   15
THE HILL   16
COMING TO THIS   17

II   *Black Maps*

THE SLEEP   21
BLACK MAPS   22
SEVEN POEMS   24
FROM A LITANY   26
THE RECOVERY   28

Contents

THE PREDICTION 29

THE ONE SONG 30

THE STONE 31

FROM A LITANY 32

III *My Life By Somebody Else*

MY LIFE 37

MY DEATH 39

MY LIFE BY SOMEBODY ELSE 40

COURTSHIP 41

ELEGY 1969 42

"THE DREADFUL HAS ALREADY HAPPENED" 43

NOT DYING 44

THE WAY IT IS 45

I

Giving Myself Up

The New Poetry Handbook

for Greg Orr and Greg Simon

1   If a man understands a poem,
      he shall have troubles.

2   If a man lives with a poem,
      he shall die lonely.

3   If a man lives with two poems,
      he shall be unfaithful to one.

4   If a man conceives of a poem,
      he shall have one less child.

5   If a man conceives of two poems,
      he shall have two children less.

6   If a man wears a crown on his head as he writes,
      he shall be found out.

7   If a man wears no crown on his head as he writes,
      he shall deceive no one but himself.

8   If a man gets angry at a poem,
      he shall be scorned by men.

9   If a man continues to be angry at a poem,
      he shall be scorned by women.

10   If a man publicly denounces poetry,
      his shoes will fill with urine.

11   If a man gives up poetry for power,
      he shall have lots of power.

12 If a man brags about his poems,
     he shall be loved by fools.

13 If a man brags about his poems and loves fools,
     he shall write no more.

14 If a man denies his poems pleasure,
     his wit shall wear boots.

15 If a man craves attention because of his poems,
     he shall be like a jackass in moonlight.

16 If a man writes a poem and praises the poem of a
                                       fellow,
     he shall have a beautiful mistress.

17 If a man writes a poem and praises the poem of a
                                    fellow overly,
     he shall drive his mistress away.

18 If a man claims the poem of another,
     his heart shall double in size.

19 If a man lets his poems go naked,
     he shall fear death.

20 If a man fears death,
     he shall be saved by his poems.

21 If a man does not fear death,
     he may or may not be saved by his poems.

22 If a man finishes a poem,
     he shall bathe in the blank wake of his passion
     and be kissed by white paper.

Breath

When you see them
tell them I am still here,
that I stand on one leg while the other one dreams,
that this is the only way,

that the lies I tell them are different
from the lies I tell myself,
that by being both here and beyond
I am becoming a horizon,

that as the sun rises and sets I know my place,
that breath is what saves me,
that even the forced syllables of decline are breath,
that if the body is a coffin it is also a closet of breath,

that breath is a mirror clouded by words,
that breath is all that survives the cry for help
as it enters the stranger's ear
and stays long after the word is gone,

that breath is the beginning again, that from it
all resistance falls away, as meaning falls
away from life, or darkness falls from light,
that breath is what I give them when I send my love.

Letter

for Richard Howard

Men are running across a field,
pens fall from their pockets.
People out walking will pick them up.
It is one of the ways letters are written.

How things fall to others!
The self no longer belonging to me, but asleep
in a stranger's shadow, now clothing
the stranger, now leading him off.

It is noon as I write to you.
Someone's life has come into my hands.
The sun whitens the buildings.
It is all I have. I give it all to you. Yours,

Giving Myself Up

I give up my eyes which are glass eggs.
I give up my tongue.
I give up my mouth which is the constant dream of my
tongue.
I give up my throat which is the sleeve of my voice.
I give up my heart which is a burning apple.
I give up my lungs which are trees that have never seen
the moon.
I give up my smell which is that of a stone traveling through
rain.
I give up my hands which are ten wishes.
I give up my arms which have wanted to leave me anyway.
I give up my legs which are lovers only at night.
I give up my buttocks which are the moons of childhood.
I give up my penis which whispers encouragement to my
thighs.
I give up my clothes which are walls that blow in the wind
and I give up the ghost that lives in them.
I give up. I give up.
And you will have none of it because already I am beginning
again without anything.

Tomorrow

Your best friend is gone,
your other friend, too.
Now the dream that used to turn in your sleep,
like a diamond, sails into the year's coldest night.

What did you say?
Or was it something you did?
It makes no difference—the house of breath collapsing
around your voice, your voice burning, are nothing to
    worry about.

Tomorrow your friends will come back;
your moist open mouth will bloom in the glass of
    storefronts.
Yes. Yes. Tomorrow they will come back and you
will invent an ending that comes out right.

The Room

It is an old story, the way it happens
sometimes in winter, sometimes not.
The listener falls to sleep,
the doors to the closets of his unhappiness open

and into his room the misfortunes come—
death by daybreak, death by nightfall,
their wooden wings bruising the air,
their shadows the spilled milk the world cries over.

There is a need for surprise endings;
the green field where cows burn like newsprint,
where the farmer sits and stares,
where nothing, when it happens, is never terrible enough.

Nostalgia

for Donald Justice

The professors of English have taken their gowns
to the laundry, have taken themselves to the fields.
Dreams of motion circle the Persian rug in a room you
    were in.
On the beach the sadness of gramophones
deepens the ocean's folding and falling.
It is yesterday. It is still yesterday.

The Remains

for Bill and Sandy Bailey

I empty myself of the names of others. I empty my pockets.
I empty my shoes and leave them beside the road.
At night I turn back the clocks;
I open the family album and look at myself as a boy.

What good does it do? The hours have done their job.
I say my own name. I say goodbye.
The words follow each other downwind.
I love my wife but send her away.

My parents rise out of their thrones
into the milky rooms of clouds. How can I sing?
Time tells me what I am. I change and I am the same.
I empty myself of my life and my life remains.

The Dance

The ghost of another comes to visit and we hold
communion while the light shines.
While the light shines, what else can we do?
And who doesn't have one foot in the grave?

I notice how the trees seem shaggy with leaves
and the steam of insects engulfs them.
The light falls like an anchor through the branches.
And which one of us is not being pulled down constantly?

My mind floats in the purple air of my skull.
I see myself dancing. I smile at everybody.
Slowly I dance out of the burning house of my head.
And who isn't borne again and again into heaven?

The Good Life

You stand at the window.
There is a glass cloud in the shape of a heart.
There are the wind's sighs that are like caves in your
    speech.
You are the ghost in the tree outside.

The street is quiet.
The weather, like tomorrow, like your life,
is partially here, partially up in the air.
There is nothing you can do.

The good life gives no warning.
It weathers the climates of despair
and appears, on foot, unrecognized, offering nothing,
and you are there.

The Dress

Lie down on the bright hill
with the moon's hand on your cheek,
your flesh deep in the white folds of your dress,
and you will not hear the passionate mole
extending the length of his darkness,
or the owl arranging all of the night,
which is his wisdom, or the poem
filling your pillow with its blue feathers.
But if you step out of your dress and move into the shade,
the mole will find you, so will the owl, and so will the poem,
and you will fall into another darkness, one you will find
yourself making and remaking until it is perfect.

The Guardian

The sun setting. The lawns on fire.
The lost day, the lost light.
Why do I love what fades?

You who left, who were leaving,
what dark rooms do you inhabit?
Guardian of my death,

preserve my absence. I am alive.

The Hill

I have come this far on my own legs,
missing the bus, missing taxis,
climbing always. One foot in front of the other,
that is the way I do it.

It does not bother me, the way the hill goes on.
Grass beside the road, a tree rattling
its black leaves. So what?
The longer I walk, the farther I am from everything.

One foot in front of the other. The hours pass.
One foot in front of the other. The years pass.
The colors of arrival fade.
That is the way I do it.

Coming to This

We have done what we wanted.
We have discarded dreams, preferring the heavy industry
of each other, and we have welcomed grief
and called ruin the impossible habit to break.

And now we are here.
The dinner is ready and we cannot eat.
The meat sits in the white lake of its dish.
The wine waits.

Coming to this
has its rewards: nothing is promised, nothing is taken
    away.
We have no heart or saving grace,
no place to go, no reason to remain.

II

Black Maps

The Sleep

There is the sleep of my tongue
speaking a language I can never remember—
words that enter the sleep of words
once they are spoken.

There is the sleep of one moment
inside the next, lengthening the night,
and the sleep of the window
turning the tall sleep of trees into glass.

The sleep of novels as they are read is soundless
like the sleep of dresses on the warm bodies of women.
And the sleep of thunder gathering dust on sunny days
and the sleep of ashes long after.

The sleep of wind has been known to fill the sky.
The long sleep of air locked in the lungs of the dead.
The sleep of a room with someone inside it.
Even the wooden sleep of the moon is possible.

And there is the sleep that demands I lie down
and be fitted to the dark that comes upon me
like another skin in which I shall never be found,
out of which I shall never appear.

Black Maps

Not the attendance of stones,
nor the applauding wind,
shall let you know
you have arrived,

nor the sea that celebrates
only departures,
nor the mountains,
nor the dying cities.

Nothing will tell you
where you are.
Each moment is a place
you've never been.

You can walk
believing you cast
a light around you.
But how will you know?

The present is always dark.
Its maps are black,
rising from nothing,
describing,

in their slow ascent
into themselves,
their own voyage,
its emptiness,

the bleak, temperate
necessity of its completion.
As they rise into being
they are like breath.

And if they are studied at all
it is only to find,
too late, what you thought
were concerns of yours

do not exist.
Your house is not marked
on any of them,
nor are your friends,

waiting for you to appear,
nor are your enemies,
listing your faults.
Only you are there,

saying hello
to what you will be,
and the black grass
is holding up the black stars.

Seven Poems

for Antonia

1

At the edge
of the body's night
ten moons are rising.

2

A scar remembers the wound.
The wound remembers the pain.
Once more you are crying.

3

When we walk in the sun
our shadows are like barges of silence.

4

My body lies down
and I hear my own
voice lying next to me.

5

The rock is pleasure
and it opens
and we enter it
as we enter ourselves
each night.

6

When I talk to the window
I say everything
is everything.

7

I have a key
so I open the door and walk in.
It is dark and I walk in.
It is darker and I walk in.

From a Litany

There in an open field I lie down in a hole I once dug and
    I praise the sky.
I praise the clouds that are like lungs of light.
I praise the owl that wants to inhabit me and the hawk that
    does not.
I praise the mouse's fury, the wolf's consideration.
I praise the dog that lives in the household of people and
    shall never be one of them.
I praise the whale that lives under the cold blankets of salt.
I praise the formations of squid, the domes of meandra.
I praise the secrecy of doors, the openness of windows.
I praise the depth of closets.
I praise the wind, the rising generations of air.
I praise the trees on whose branches shall sit the Cock of
    Portugal and the Polish Cock.
I praise the palm trees of Rio and those that shall grow in
    London.
I praise the gardeners, the worms and the small plants that
    praise each other.
I praise the sweet berries of Georgetown, Maine and the
    song of the white-throated sparrow.
I praise the poets of Waverly Place and Eleventh Street,
    and the one whose bones turn to dark emeralds when
    he stands upright in the wind.
I praise the clocks for which I grow old in a day and young
    in a day.
I praise all manner of shade, that which I see and that
    which I do not.

I praise all roofs from the watery roof of the pond to the
    slate roof of the customs house.
I praise those who have made of their bodies final embassies
    of flesh.
I praise the failure of those with ambition, the authors of
    leaflets and notebooks of nothing.
I praise the moon for suffering men.
I praise the sun its tributes.
I praise the pain of revival and the bliss of decline.
I praise all for nothing because there is no price.
I praise myself for the way I have with a shovel and I praise
    the shovel.
I praise the motive of praise by which I shall be reborn.
I praise the morning whose sun is upon me.
I praise the evening whose son I am.

The Recovery

I stood alone in the weather
and wished I were wrapped in the stones,
the long sheets, the bones of my father
laid out in the ground, and later,

after waiting, and watching
the sun fall into the hills and the night
close down over the least light,
I walked to the water's edge

and saw the doctors wave from the deck of a boat
that steamed from port, their bags open,
their instruments shining like ruins under the moon,
and it was no more than anyone might have predicted.

The Prediction

That night the moon drifted over the pond,
turning the water to milk, and under
the boughs of the trees, the blue trees,
a young woman walked, and for an instant

the future came to her:
rain falling on her husband's grave, rain falling
on the lawns of her children, her own mouth
filling with cold air, strangers moving into her house,

a man in her room writing a poem, the moon drifting
        into it,
a woman strolling under its trees, thinking of death,
thinking of him thinking of her, and the wind rising
and taking the moon and leaving the paper dark.

The One Song

I prefer to sit all day
like a sack in a chair
and to lie all night
like a stone in my bed.

When food comes
I open my mouth.
When sleep comes
I close my eyes.

My body sings
only one song;
the wind turns
gray in my arms.

Flowers bloom.
Flowers die.
More is less.
I long for more.

The Stone

The stone lives on.
The followers of the man with the glass face
walk around it
with their glass legs
and glass arms.

The stone lives on.
It lives on air.
It lives on your looking.
It lives inside and outside
itself and is never clear
which is which.

That is why
the followers of the man with the glass face
walk around it proposing
the possibilities
of emptiness.

The stone lives on,
commending itself to the hardness of air,
to the long meadows of your looking.

From a Litany

Let the shark keep to the shelves and closets of coral.
Let cats throw over their wisdom.
Let the noble horse who rocks under the outlaw's ass eat
plastic turf.
For no creature is safe.
Let the great sow of state grow strong.
Let those in office search under their clothes for the private
life.
They will find nothing.
Let them gather together and hold hands.
They shall have nothing to hold.
Let the flag flutter in the glass moon of each eye.
Let the black-suited priests stand for the good life.
Let them tell us to be more like them.
For that is the nature of the sickness.
Let the bodies of debutantes gleam like frigidaires.
For they shall have sex with food.
Let flies sink into their mothers' thighs and go blind in the
trenches of meat.
Let the patient unmask the doctor and swim in the gray
milk of his mind.
For nothing will keep.
Let the bleak faces of the police swell like yeast.
Let breezes run like sauce over their skins.
For this kingdom is theirs.
Let a violet cloak fall on the bleached hair of the poetess.

Let twilight cover the lost bone of her passion.
For her moon is ambition.
Let the dusty air release its sugars.
Let candy the color of marlin flesh build up on the tables.
For everyone's mouth is open.
Let the wind devise secrets and leave them in trees.
Let the earth suck at roots and discover the emblems of
      weather.

III

My Life By Somebody Else

My Life

The huge doll of my body
refuses to rise.
I am the toy of women.
My mother

would prop me up for her friends.
"Talk, talk," she would beg.
I moved my mouth
but words did not come.

My wife took me down from the shelf.
I lay in her arms. "We suffer
the sickness of self," she would whisper.
And I lay there dumb.

Now my daughter
gives me a plastic nurser
filled with water.
"You are my real baby," she says.

Poor child!
I look into the brown
mirrors of her eyes
and see myself

diminishing, sinking down
to a depth she does not know is there.
Out of breath,
I will not rise again.

I grow into my death.
My life is small
and getting smaller. The world is green.
Nothing is all.

My Death

Sadness, of course, and confusion.
The relatives gathered at the graveside,
talking about the waste, and the weather mounting,
the rain moving in vague pillars offshore.

This is Prince Edward Island.
I came back to my birthplace to announce my death.
I said I would ride full gallop into the sea
and not look back. People were furious.

I told them about attempts I had made in the past,
how I starved in order to be the size of Lucille,
whom I loved, to inhabit the cold space
her body had taken. They were shocked.

I went on about the time
I dove in a perfect arc that filled
with the sunshine of farewell and I fell
head over shoulders into the river's thigh.

And about the time
I stood naked in the snow, pointing a pistol
between my eyes, and how when I fired my head bloomed
into health. Soon I was alone.

Now I lie in the box
of my making while the weather
builds and the mourners shake their heads as if
to write or to die, I did not have to do either.

My Life By Somebody Else

I have done what I could but you avoid me.
I left a bowl of milk on the desk to tempt you.
Nothing happened. I left my wallet there, full of money.
You must have hated me for that. You never came.

I sat at my typewriter naked, hoping you would wrestle me
to the floor. I played with myself just to arouse you.
Boredom drove me to sleep. I offered you my wife.
I sat her on the desk and spread her legs. I waited.

The days drag on. The exhausted light falls like a bandage
over my eyes. Is it because I am ugly? Was anyone
ever so sad? It is pointless to slash my wrists. My hands
would fall off. And then what hope would I have?

Why do you never come? Must I have you by being
somebody else? Must I write *My Life* by somebody else?
My Death by somebody else? Are you listening?
Somebody else has arrived. Somebody else is writing.

Courtship

There is a girl you like so you tell her
your penis is big, but that you cannot get yourself
to use it. Its demands are ridiculous, you say,
even self-defeating, but to be honored somehow,
briefly, inconspicuously in the dark.

When she closes her eyes in horror,
you take it all back. You tell her you're almost
a girl yourself and can understand why she is shocked.
When she is about to walk away, you tell her
you have no penis, that you don't

know what got into you. You get on your knees.
She suddenly bends down to kiss your shoulder and you
    know
you're on the right track. You tell her you want
to bear children and that is why you seem confused.
You wrinkle your brow and curse the day you were born.

She tries to calm you, but you lose control.
You reach for her panties and beg forgiveness as you do.
She squirms and you howl like a wolf. Your craving
seems monumental. You know you will have her.
Taken by storm, she is the girl you will marry.

Elegy 1969

You slave away into your old age
and nothing you do adds up to much.
Day after day you go through the same motions,
you shiver in bed, you get hungry, you want a woman.

Heroes standing for lives of sacrifice and obedience
fill the parks through which you walk.
At night in the fog they open their bronze umbrellas
or else withdraw to the empty lobbies of movie houses.

You love the night for its power of annihilating,
but while you sleep, your problems will not let you die.
Waking only proves the existence of The Great Machine
and the hard light falls on your shoulders.

You walk among the dead and talk
about times to come and matters of the spirit.
Literature wasted your best hours of love-making.
Weekends were lost, cleaning your apartment.

You are quick to confess your failure and to postpone
collective joy to the next century. You accept
rain, war, unemployment and the unjust distribution of
    wealth
because you can't, all by yourself, blow up Manhattan
    Island.

(AFTER CARLOS DRUMMOND DE ANDRADE)

"The Dreadful Has Already Happened"

The relatives are leaning over, staring expectantly.
They moisten their lips with their tongues. I can feel
them urging me on. I hold the baby in the air.
Heaps of broken bottles glitter in the sun.

A small band is playing old fashioned marches.
My mother is keeping time by stamping her foot.
My father is kissing a woman who keeps waving
to somebody else. There are palm trees.

The hills are spotted with orange flamboyants and tall
billowy clouds move behind them. "Go on, Boy,"
I hear somebody say, "Go on."
I keep wondering if it will rain.

The sky darkens. There is thunder.
"Break his legs," says one of my aunts,
"Now give him a kiss." I do what I'm told.
The trees bend in the bleak tropical wind.

The baby did not scream, but I remember that sigh
when I reached inside for his tiny lungs and shook them
out in the air for the flies. The relatives cheered.
It was about that time I gave up.

Now, when I answer the phone, his lips
are in the receiver; when I sleep, his hair is gathered
around a familiar face on the pillow; wherever I search
I find his feet. He is what is left of my life.

Not Dying

These wrinkles are nothing.
These gray hairs are nothing.
This stomach which sags
with old food, these bruised
and swollen ankles,
my darkening brain,
they are nothing.
I am the same boy
my mother used to kiss.

The years change nothing.
On windless summer nights
I feel those kisses
slide from her dark
lips far away,
and in winter they float
over the frozen pines
and arrive covered with snow.
They keep me young.

My passion for milk
is uncontrollable still.
I am driven by innocence.
From bed to chair I crawl
and back again.
I shall not die.
The grave result
and token of birth, my body
remembers and holds fast.

The Way It Is

The world is ugly
And the people are sad.
WALLACE STEVENS

I lie in bed.
I toss all night
in the cold unruffled deep
of my sheets and cannot sleep.

My neighbor marches in his room,
wearing the sleek
mask of a hawk with a large beak.
He stands by the window. A violet plume

rises from his helmet's dome.
The moon's light
spills over him like milk and the wind rinses the white
glass bowls of his eyes.

His helmet in a shopping bag,
he sits in the park, waving a small American flag.
He cannot be heard as he moves
behind trees and hedges,

always at the frayed edges
of town, pulling a gun on someone like me. I crouch
under the kitchen table, telling myself
I am a dog, who would kill a dog?

My neighbor's wife comes home.
She walks into the living room,
takes off her clothes, her hair falls down her back.
She seems to wade

through long flat rivers of shade.
The soles of her feet are black.
She kisses her husband's neck
and puts her hands inside his pants.

My neighbors dance.
They roll on the floor, his tongue
is in her ear, his lungs
reek with the swill and weather of hell.

Out on the street people are lying down
with their knees in the air, tears
fill their eyes, ashes
enter their ears.

Their clothes are torn
from their backs. Their faces are worn.
Horsemen are riding around them, telling them why
they should die.

My neighbor's wife calls to me, her mouth is pressed
against the wall behind my bed.
She says, "My husband's dead."
I turn over on my side,

hoping she has not lied.
The walls and ceiling of my room are gray—
the moon's color through the windows of a laundromat.
I close my eyes.

I see myself float
on the dead sea of my bed, falling away.
calling for help, but the vague scream
sticks in my throat.

I see myself in the park
on horseback, surrounded by dark,
leading the armies of peace.
The iron legs of the horse do not bend.

I drop the reins. Where will the turmoil end?
Fleets of taxis stall
in the fog, passengers fall
asleep. Gas pours

from a tri-colored stack.
Locking their doors,
people from offices huddle together,
telling the same story over and over.

Everyone who has sold himself wants to buy himself back.
Nothing is done. The night
eats into their limbs
like a blight.

Everything dims.
The future is not what it used to be.
The graves are ready. The dead
shall inherit the dead.

Mark Strand was born in Summerside, Prince Edward Island, Canada. He lives in New York and is a visiting lecturer at Yale University. His previous books of poems are "Sleeping With One Eye Open" (1964) and "Reasons For Moving" (1968).